CW00839561

What Am I?

Kasia Reay

Illustrated by Rachel Hudson

Schofield&Sims

What is this mess? Can you sort it all out?

My long back legs help me to hop and swim. I do not have a tail. What am I?

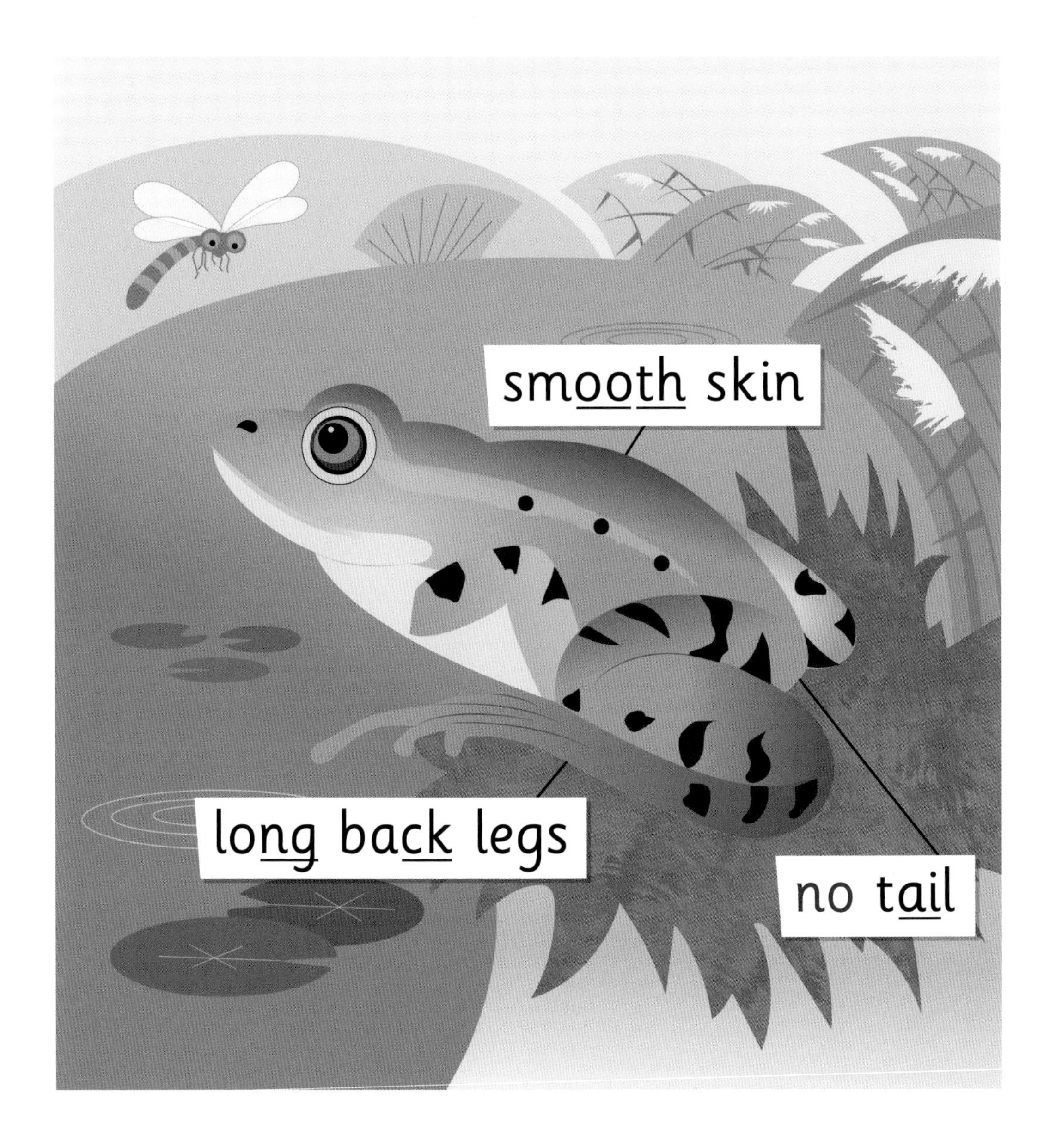
smooth skin
long back legs
no tail

Frogs swim in ponds and hop on land. Insects, snails and slugs are all food for frogs.

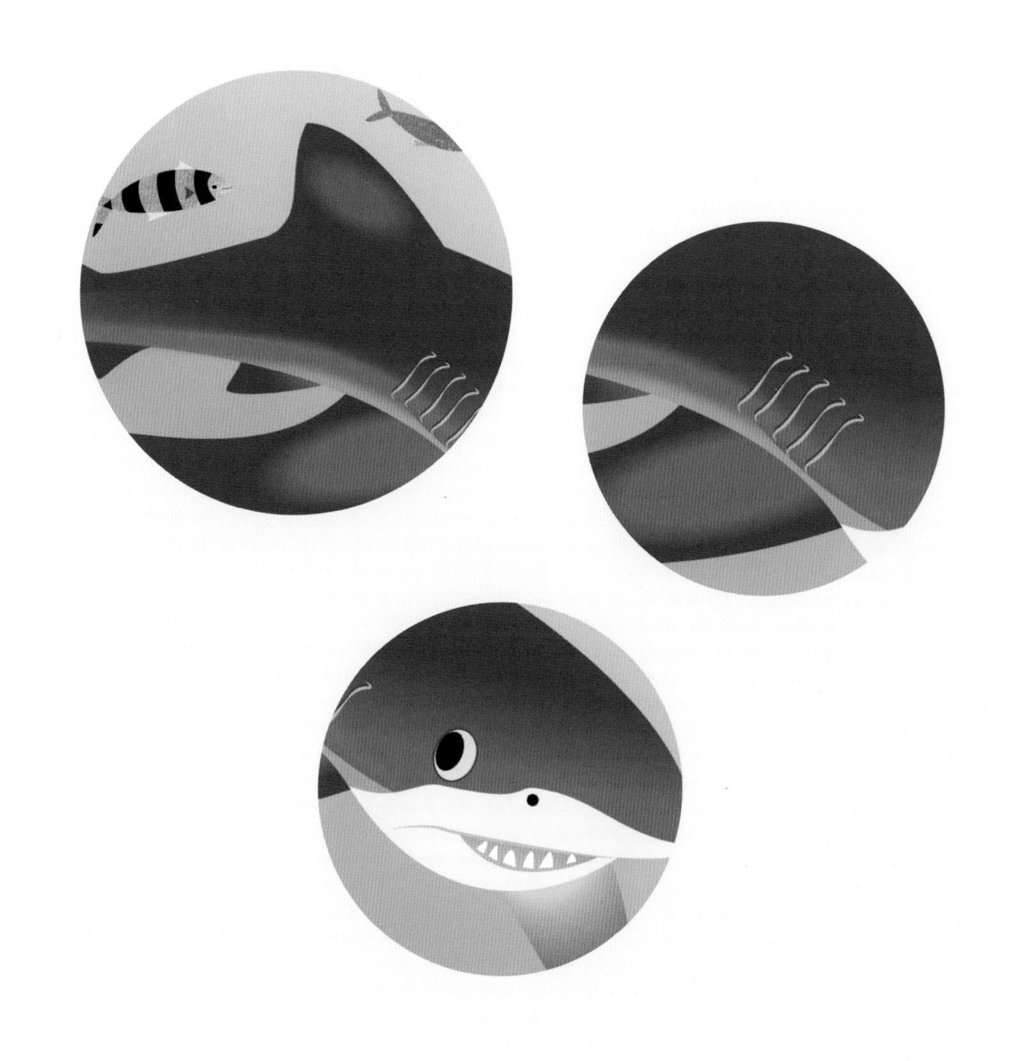

I have fins and gills. I have lots of sharp teeth. What am I?

fin
gill
sharp teeth

Sharks like to hunt at night. Good hearing helps them hunt for food.

I am soft, but I have a hard shell.
I have one flat foot. What am I?

hard shell
flat foot

Snails like to come out when it is wet. A snail curls back into its shell to sleep.

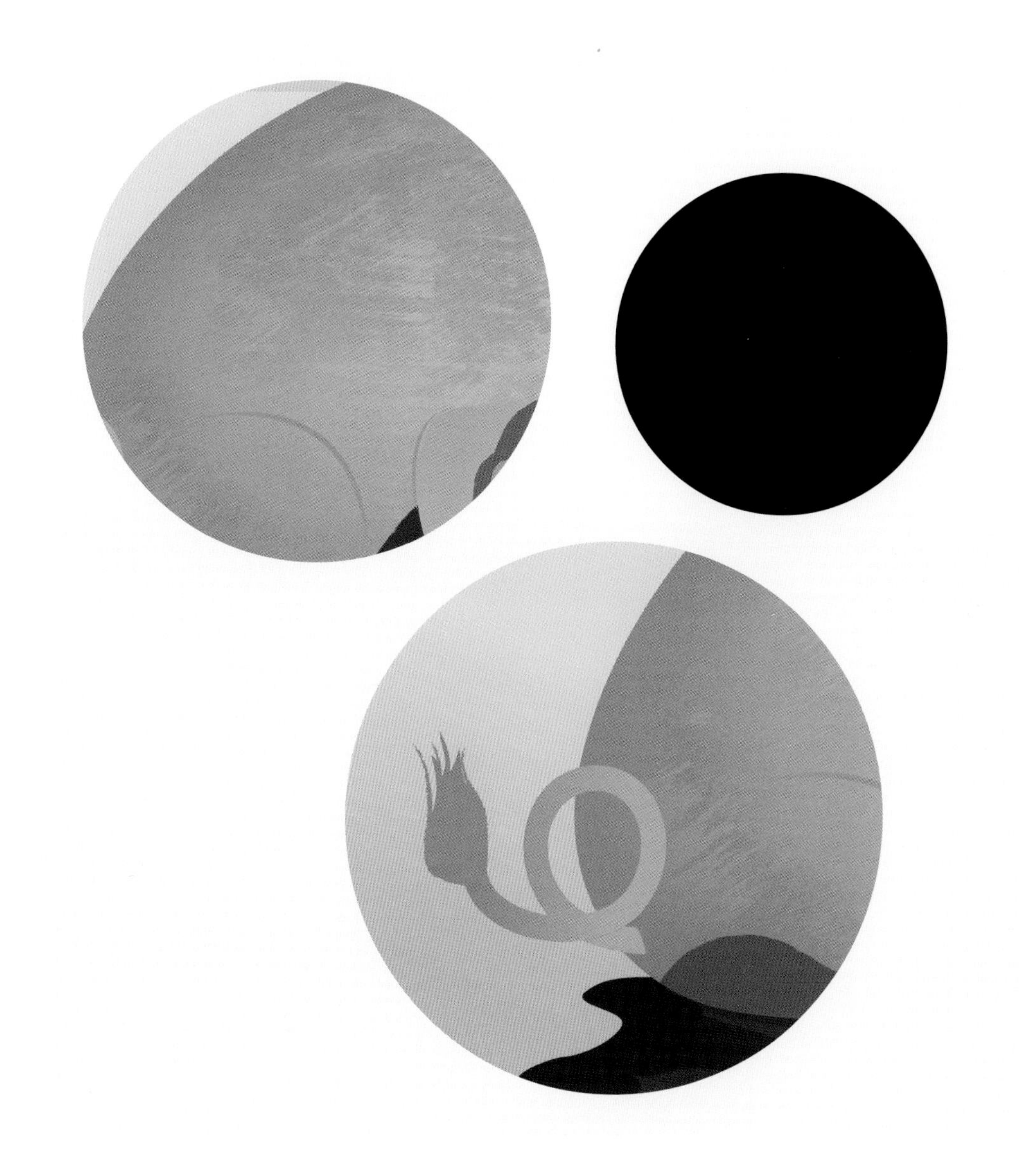

We have pink or black skin. We have tails that curl. What are we?

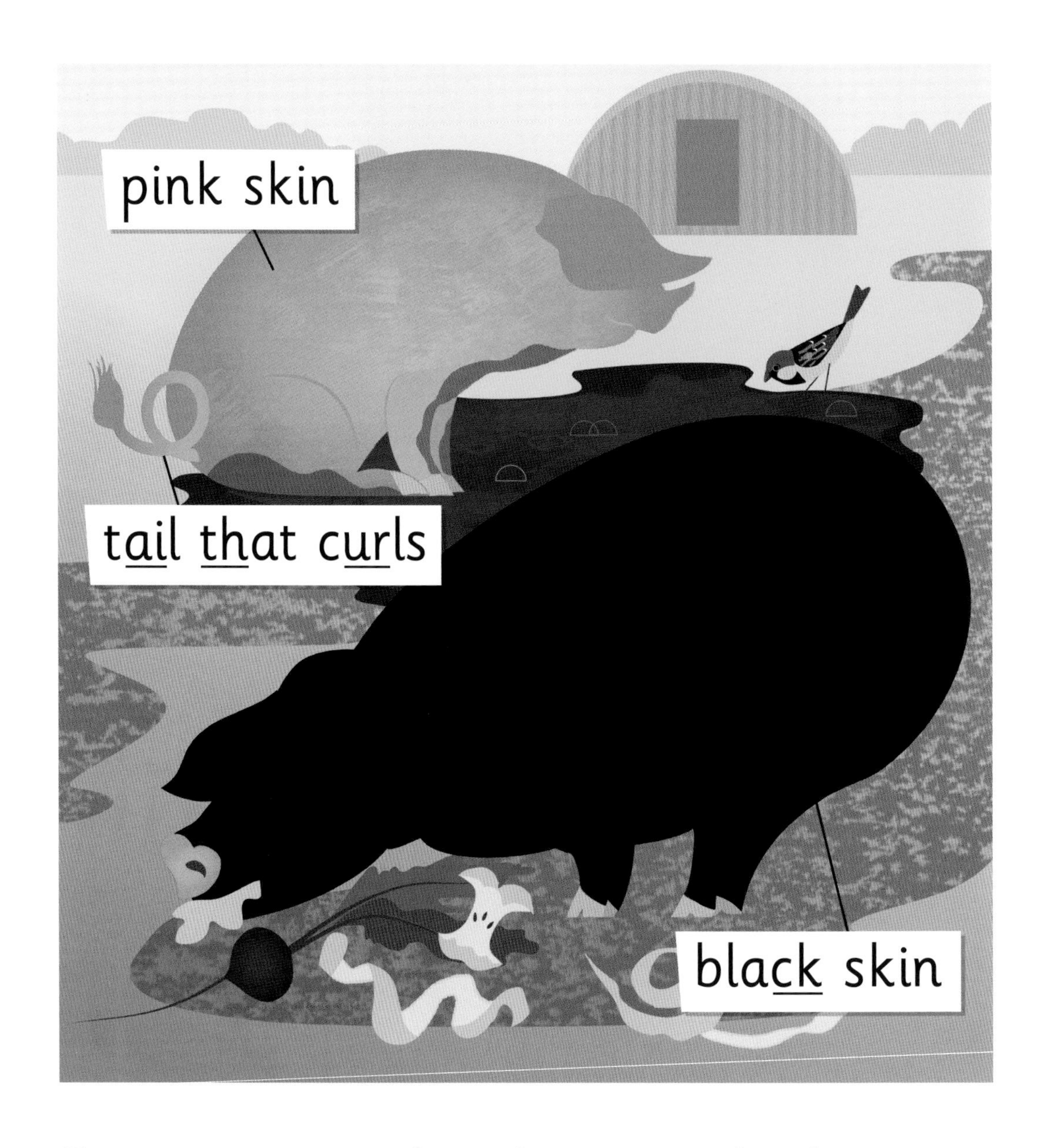
pink skin
tail that curls
black skin

Pigs go in mud to keep cool when it is hot. Pigs can smell and hear better than they can see.

Some of us look like we have spots of black paint on us! We have pink udders for milk. What are we?

Cows munch on green grass. A lot of the milk we drink comes from cows.